The Divali Party

Written by Lisa Bruce
Illustrated by Julie Banyard

Collins *Educational*
An imprint of HarperCollins*Publishers*

The Patels were busy.
"What are you doing?" asked Mrs Walker.
"We're getting the house ready for Divali," said Mrs Patel.

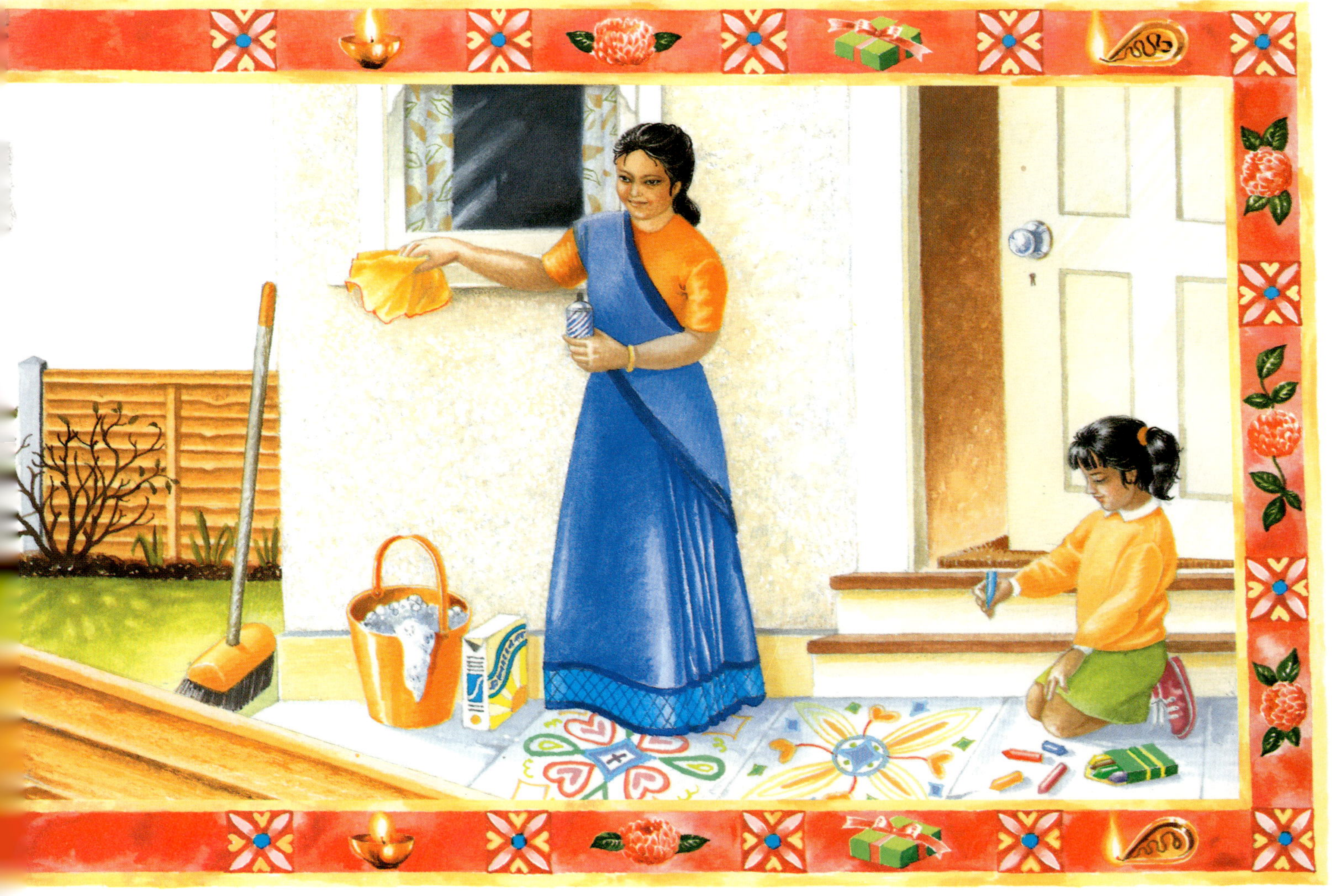

"That's a lovely smell," said Ellie.
"I'm making sweets for Divali," said Mr Patel.

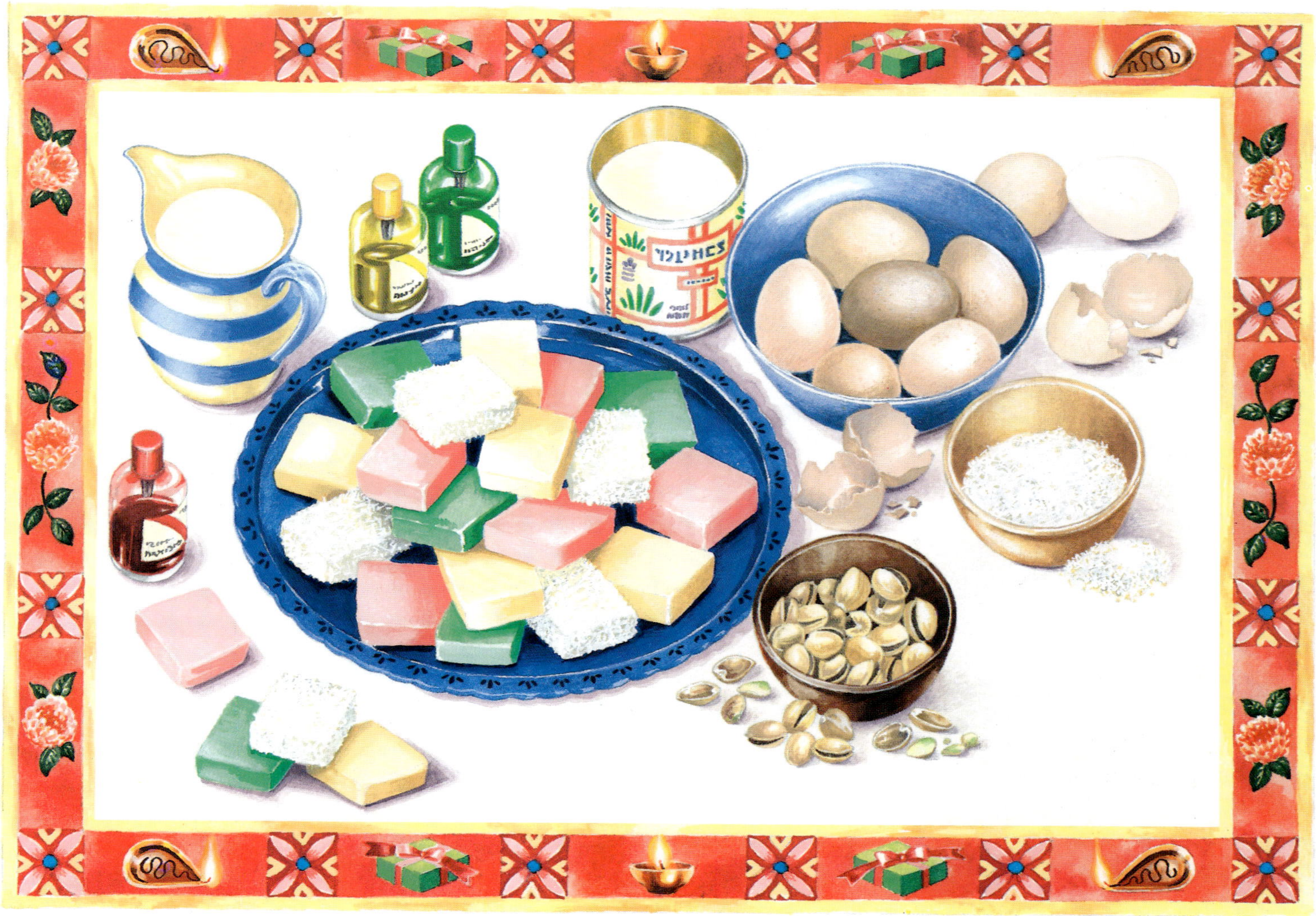

"What are all those little candles?" asked Jim. "We call them divas," said Anil. "They're for Divali, our festival of light."

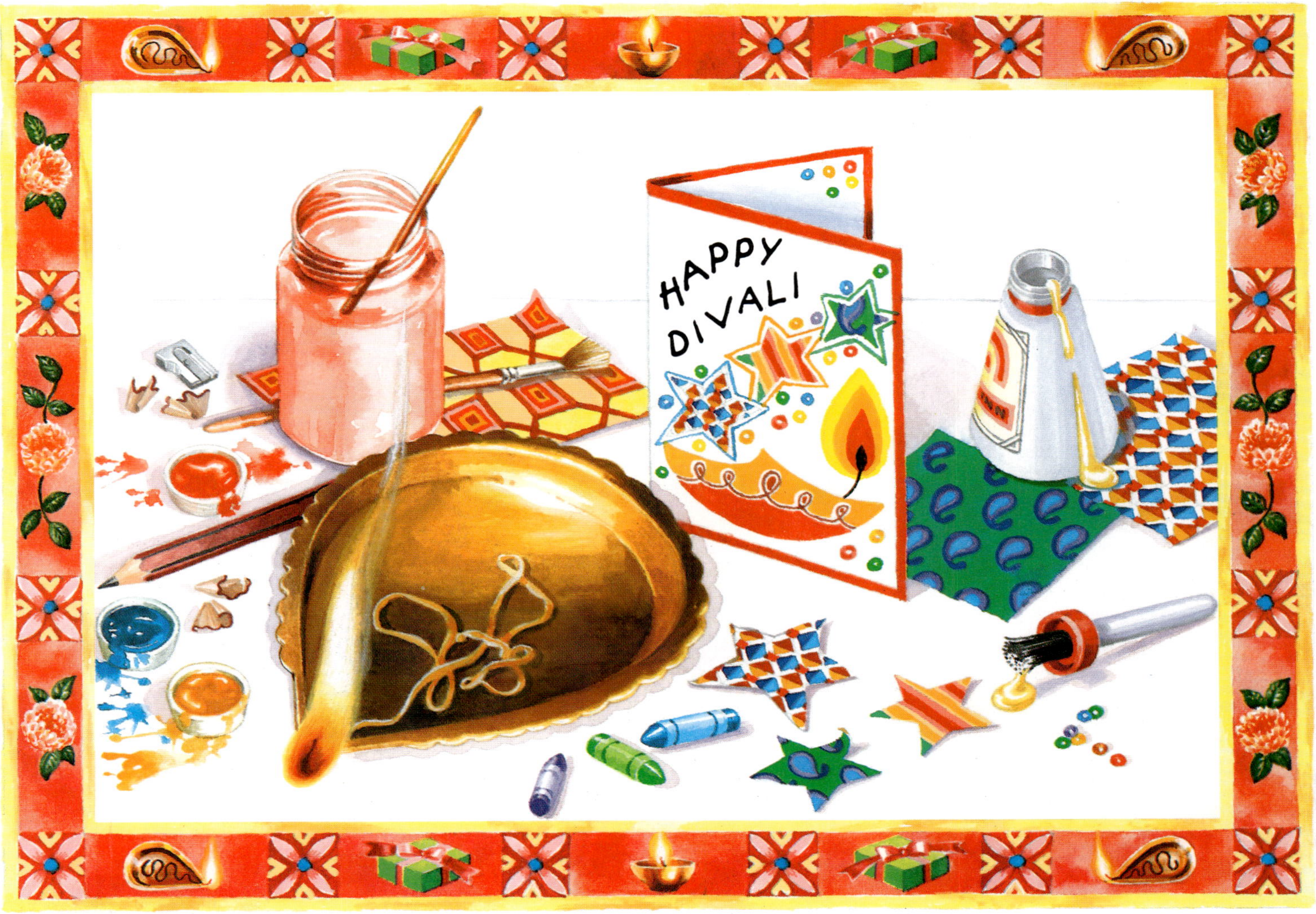
HAPPY
DIVALI

In the evening, the Divali celebrations began and Anil lit all the divas. Family and friends came to visit.

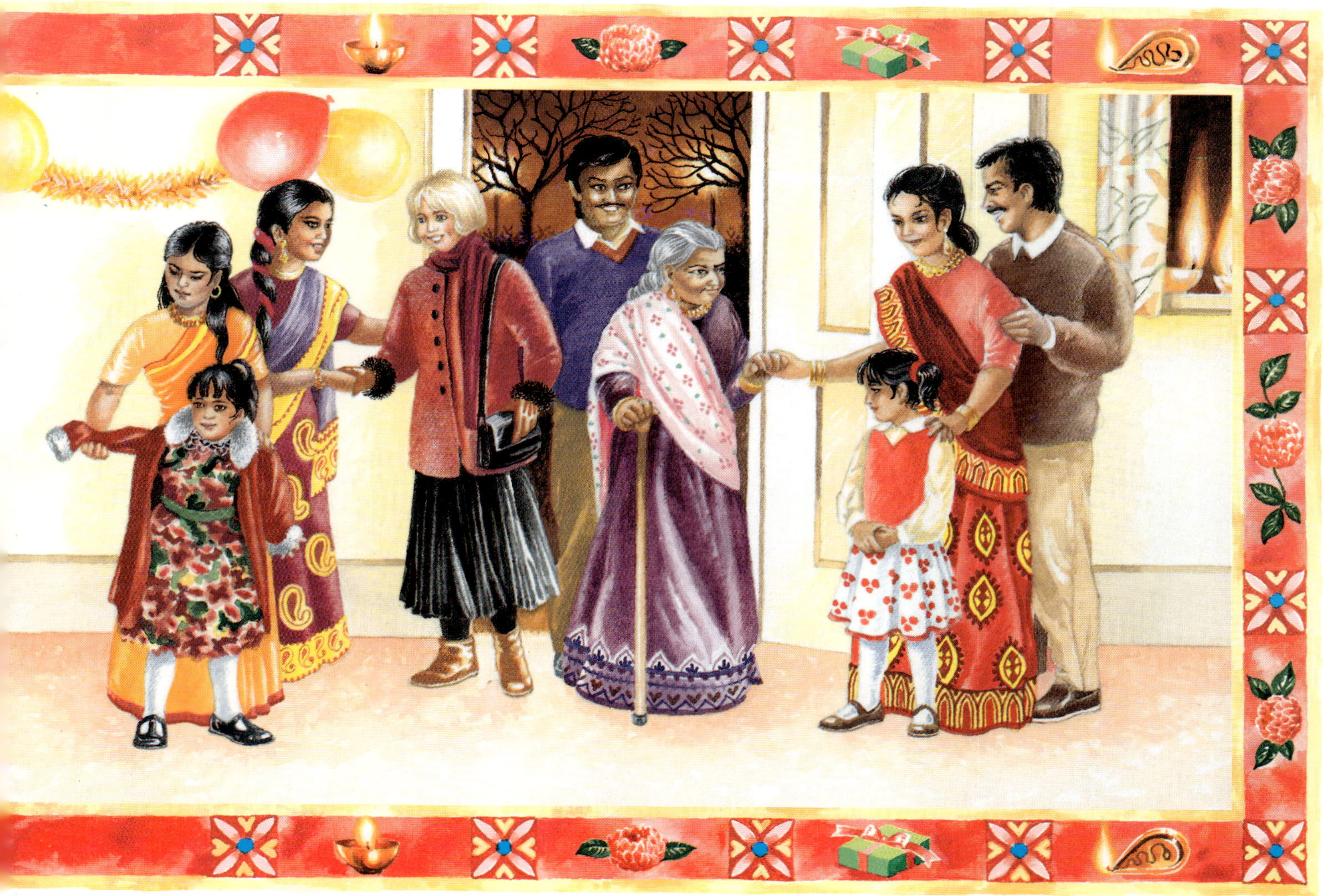

Nani told the children the story of Rama and Sita.

Then they all sat down to eat.

Just then the
doorbell rang.
It was Mrs Walker,
Ellie, and Jim.

"There's been a powercut," they said to Mrs Patel. "Yours is the only house with lights."

"Come in and join our Divali Party," said Mrs Patel.

15

Facts about Divali

Divali is the Hindu festival of light. It is usually celebrated in November and lasts for five days. Hindus light divas to welcome the goddess, Lakshmi. They hope that she will bring them good health and happiness. They also celebrate the return of Rama and Sita to their homeland. Try and find a book to read about the legend of Rama and Sita.

Hindus send Divali cards and make sweets out of sugar, pistachio nuts and condensed milk to give to their family and friends. They also decorate their doorsteps with Rangoli patterns. These are made from coloured paint, card and even rice.

At Divali, Hindus wear gold jewellery and new clothes. They often wear red because this colour is supposed to bring good luck. The women make patterns on their hands with a red dye called henna.

Nani is the Hindu name for Grandmother.